Betty-Lo
THAN
TEACH ~~~ ~~~ ~~~
COMMITMENT TO STUDENTS.

For Those Who
Dare to Teach

THANKS ALSO FOR BEING A
WONDERFUL FRIEND WHO HAS
TAUGHT ME MUCH.

LOVE,
Billy Strean

Billy Strean, Ph.D.

Professor and 3M National Teaching Fellow

ISBN-10:1973779625
ISBN-13: 978-1973779629

DEDICATION

To all those who dare to teach.

CONTENTS

ACKNOWLEDGMENTS

Thank you to all the wonderful teachers who have made me who I am today, and who provided models, practices, and humanity for me to emulate. Thank you to all the amazing students who have allowed me the opportunity to make a difference with you and who have taught me so much about how to be a teacher. Thank you to my family and friends who have supported me and given joy and richness to my life. Thank you to everyone and everything that has caused me to laugh and learn. I love you all.

Preface

Venturing into teaching may require certification, but much of what it takes to be skillful and successful is not taught in school. In this book, from my 35 years of teaching and coaching, I share stories and insights in which I hope you will find wisdom and practical suggestions.

Sometimes our greatest skills and contributions become invisible to us. Many of us come from or live in cultures where we have learned that claiming and voicing our gifts is not appropriate. In the realm of Canadian niceties, I've learned that although I've received national recognition for teaching and educational leadership, I should keep a low profile. It is here that I draw wisdom from Marianne Williamson, "Your playing small does not serve the world. There is nothing enlightened about shrinking so that other people won't feel insecure around you. We are all meant to shine, as children do … as we let our own light shine, we unconsciously give others permission to do the same. As we are liberated from our own fear, our presence automatically liberates others."

In an effort to let go of fear and to offer you greater freedom, please allow me to shed the perspective of scholar/academic espousing information about various factors in teaching and please let me "play big" in an effort to serve the world by owning my experience and excellence as a teacher. As Marianne led into the previous quotation, ""Our deepest fear is not that we are inadequate. Our deepest fear is that we are powerful beyond measure.

It is our light, not our darkness that most frightens us. We ask ourselves, Who am I to be brilliant, gorgeous, talented, fabulous? Actually, who are you *not* to be?"

Let's face the light together as I share my stories with the intention of helping you to be inspired and to shine most brightly as a teacher (coach, parent, leader, person).

You are enough. Be more.

If you resonate with any of the broadest aspects of "those who dare to teach," then you may have wrestled with questions about with whom you should share your gifts and how you might best contribute. This has been one of my great self-generated and self-perpetuating challenges. Like many who have been trained to use their intellect rather than their intuition or deeper knowing, I've tried to *figure out* these issues of audience and undertakings. Perhaps from frustration or fatigue, I shifted to "listening" and feeling and found it was more profitable to stay connected to purpose and commitment than to agonize over precise steps. This perspective is important as you step into this book. Instead of absorbing information intellectually, I invite you to assume that the ideas will largely do you little good until you act and explore. It is through your hands that you will move concepts from your head to your heart. This is a heart project. This book is about you Being a Teacher.

Introduction

This is a book of autobiographical tales associated with lessons about teaching and learning. The chapters recount experiences ranging from early childhood baseball fields to writing my part of a nomination for a national teaching award and what I discovered about teaching along the way. Each of these chapters offers some practical applications for teaching.

In Chapter 1, *Little League, Big Lessons*, you'll learn about how my experiences as a six year-old batboy shaped my views about power relations and the humanity of teaching. Chapter 2, *Everything I Need to Know about Teaching I Didn't Learn in Kindergarten*, tells how some great elementary school teachers set the stage for the value of learning outcomes and active learning. The third chapter, *A View from the Sidelines*, takes you into my first coaching adventures and suggests some ideas about clarifying your values and getting to know your students. Then, *Best Lessons from Worst Moments in College* gives some classic examples of learning what to do from the pain of poor pedagogy. In *Nothing Like Camp*, I share some great tips I got as a counselor that can help us as teachers. Chapter 6, *Lessons from Graduate School* explores a key shift for developing teachers and how I came to appreciate the dramatic aspect of teaching. The most recent story is shared in *"We Want to Nominate You": The Genesis of Exhilarated Learning*, which addresses the three dimensions of my approach: human connection, whole-body learning, and content to context. Finally, I offer three bonus chapters that introduce you to the

ALIVE model, make the case for the importance of emotions, and offer cutting edge information about goal setting and attainment to help you to implement the ideas in this book.

For Those Who Dare to Teach

1 *LITTLE LEAGUE, BIG LESSONS*

"Strike three. You're out," announced the umpire of this contest in the Teaneck T-shirt Baseball League. The coach of the victorious Yankees was disturbingly elated and the dejected faces of the boys on the defeated Astros suggested there was more at stake than the purported fun, recreation, and learning about how to play a sport.

There must be something very important about winning a Little League baseball game. Apparently it's valuable enough to crush the hearts and spirits of young boys. I was six years old and the batboy for the Astros in the Teaneck T-shirt League when I learned my first lesson about teaching. I had no idea then that was what I was learning and probably didn't realize that this experience's impact may have led me to doctoral studies in sport psychology with a dissertation about parents and coaches in youth sport. What must have hit me at a very deep level were the misuse of power and the misguided direction of what was being done for whom. This was supposed to be about the kids.

It's cliché to suggest that many of our best

practices come from *not* doing things that were most troublesome for us. Yet, it's clear to me that some of my most fervently held beliefs and most heartfelt approaches to teaching come from some of the worst experiences I've had as a learner. I've also been fortunate to have some wonderful teachers and coaches. Emulating them has given me other components of my teaching style.

Perhaps twenty-five years in Canada has given me sensibilities that make it more challenging to position myself as "one who knows" that decries my American willingness to be more rah-rah. I frequently return to Marianne Williamson's line: "there is nothing enlightened about shrinking so that other people won't feel insecure around you." (The full quotation, below, is frequently cited, yet deserves another read in the context of you as a teacher.) About six years ago, I was among ten Canadians honoured for excellence in teaching and educational leadership as a 3M National Teaching Fellow. When the other nine in my cohort unanimously put me forward as their spokesman, that should have had me fully convinced that I have something to say. It took me a couple more years for the message to sink in intellectually; viscerally I'm still wrestling with being a Sensei, or a teacher of teachers.

What I am more comfortable with is sharing my story and unfolding for you how I've come to teaching philosophies and methods that may assist you in your teaching journey. Let me say something about the scope of this book. Although I am addressing those who teach in academic settings, I draw on experiences in coaching and parenting and the ideas are applicable for educators in the broadest sense.

Our deepest fear is not that we are inadequate. Our deepest fear is that we are powerful beyond measure. It is our light, not our darkness that most frightens us. We ask ourselves, Who am I to be brilliant, gorgeous, talented, fabulous? Actually, who are you not to be? You are a child of God. Your playing small does not serve the world. There is nothing enlightened about shrinking so that other people won't feel insecure around you. We are all meant to shine, as children do. We were born to make manifest the glory of God that is within us. It's not just in some of us; it's in everyone. And as we let our own light shine, we unconsciously give other people permission to do the same. As we are liberated from our own fear, our presence automatically liberates others. (Marianne Williamson, 1992, *A Return to Love*).

Let's go back to the baseball field and uncover more of what I saw and how the foundation of my teaching was formed. My older brother, Rich, was playing in his first adult-organized sport experience and our dad was one of the coaches. I keenly wanted to be as much a part of my big brother's world as possible, so was happy to come along to the games and was tasked with serving as batboy. There's something laughable to me about how the misadventures and insanity in this milieu may have been pivotal in shaping my career choice. As a sport psychologist who focused on youth sport for many years, I've seen and heard some wild examples of "adults gone bad" around their children's fields, courts, and arenas. My observations as a first grader included their own gems: "Our" team, the Astros, was

3

pretty good. Yet, we couldn't seem to get by the Yankees. Their coach, however, didn't follow the playing time rules and kept his weaker players on the bench more than was allowed. Our best pitcher would glance over to his father after each delivery to see if he still had his approval. The emotional value of winning and losing was enormous. The outcome was tantamount. These were 8 and 9 year old boys. Fervent conversations at home addressed the inappropriateness of the adults' behaviors, yet all involved seemed quite attached to competitive results.

My young and sensitive being knew something was really wrong about all of this malarkey in a supposed recreational program for children. I saw kids being hurt and decided something about how people in positions of power must take care of those within their charge. There likely were other contributing experiences, but by the time I was 16 and began coaching and teaching, it was solidified deep within me that I will always treat those I teach with respect and dignity and do my best to recognize always that I am there for them. Perhaps my first teaching aphorism is "People don't care what you know until they know that you care."

Outside of teaching, this deeply held value creates a lot of upsets and gets me in trouble from time to time. It makes me crazy whenever I see a parent, coach, teacher, or administrator misusing power. But it is at the core of what makes me successful and a key in what I advocate for teachers.

So you've heard the story and the associated beliefs and values that emerged. What are my teaching practices that reflect these experiences? What do I do and what can you take for your work?

I have come to a frightening conclusion. I am the decisive element in the classroom. It is my personal approach that creates the climate. It is my daily mood that makes the weather. As a teacher I possess tremendous power to make a child's life miserable or joyous. I can be a tool of torture or an instrument of inspiration. I can humiliate or humor, hurt or heal. In all situations, it is my response that decides whether a crisis will be escalated or de-escalated, and a child humanized or de-humanized.
Haim Ginott (1972)

After reading that quotation and reflecting for a few moments, I want to add a comment and alter the question. I realize that the preceding story occurs to me as a bit blah-blah-blah and what interests me most is what's practically valuable. Yet, the "big secret" is that great teaching is less about what you do and more about who you are. The more useful question may be something like "who are you being?" How you show up, as a human being, is decisive. The good news and bad news here is that following the recipe for a lesson plan is a lot easier than doing what it takes to grow and develop yourself so that you show up as far down the path of caring and authenticity as possible. On the other hand, if you really care about your students and they know it, they will grant you a lot of latitude for error in your teaching. (If they assess you as phony or uncaring, however, they will pounce on your mistakes.)

Now the notion of "those who dare to teach"[1] starts to make sense. It is a grand endeavor to be the best person you can be and put yourself on an unending path of growth and development so that you can "be" an effective teacher. How do you do that?

1. **Be curious & Stay curious** – Unless you are truly fascinated by how human beings learn (especially you), this is probably a painful path. If you don' t want to "never cease to learn," then you will end up leaving the profession or causing suffering – likely for yourself and students. If you dedicate yourself to "getting it right" and give up "being right," you will find the opportunity in every failure and learn from every experience. When you notice your foibles or see something that doesn't work about how you interact with students, mine the moment for every kernel of useful information. Be your own greatest "work in progress." I've had the privilege of working with many world-class performers in sports, education, business, medicine, and the arts. It is extremely common that these folks are far less interested in kudos and intensely eager to hear anything that can make them better. (Granted it is often taken past a healthy or balanced point, but the spirit is so useful.) If you can stay unattached to the

---

[1] This comes from the quotation "Who dares to teach must never cease to learn" John Cotton Dana (1856–1929).

correctness of your positions and methods and remain inquisitive about any tweak that will assist your students' learning, you will have unlimited fun and find joy in continuous improvement.

2. **Be systematic and intentional about your personal and professional development** – This is the world of "practices." Although a positive attitude can be quite helpful, even if you don't like them, good practices shift who you are. I'll advocate meditation as an example of both sides of this suggestion. I often say I've been "wrestling with a meditation practice since 1986." I don't love it. I don't look forward to it or enjoy it the way I do fitness or yoga. But even though I'm not fully drawn to the practice, I get the benefits (and realizing I get the benefits probably keeps me coming back). Meditation is like brushing your teeth for your nervous system. We are more bombarded than ever by huge quantities of stimuli. There's enormous evidence that our brains need a rest and we get many diverse benefits from meditation. (For more information on the topic, and my ALIVE model, stayed tuned for my forthcoming book, which will give you lots of ideas and practices for your energy, relationships, purpose, connection, and enjoyment.) Too many people let their personal and professional wellness or development happen by accident. If you aren't working a plan to get better, you are

probably getting worse. Nothing stays constant. People readily acknowledge if they stop running or lifting weights, their fitness will atrophy. Your professional skills operate in the same fashion; if you don't train, you will diminish. There's a virtually endless menu of learning opportunities. Keep a steady diet.

3. **Prioritize the people** – Remember: they don't care what you know until they know that you care. To add to this point and, more generally, is the importance of your conscious use of your power as an educator: we are animals with a phenomenal system that recalls where we have experienced pain and where threat may exist in our current environment. Students intelligently recognize based on their past experiences of shame, humiliation, embarrassment, or feeling made wrong that it is not "safe" to participate in class. Simply declaring, "this is a safe place" is like telling a paranoid person that there is nothing to worry about. You need to prove it through your being and actions. It is virtually impossible for human beings to be in a state of growth, learning, and development at the same time as they are in a state of fear and protection. To be open for learning, people have to feel a sufficient sense of trust and that you are not going to hurt them. Be respectful and acknowledge that every student has at least one good reason not to participate. It didn't work out in the past and the most basic part of their brain has stored that painful

experience.

I begin every class with a conversation on the first day about our histories in classrooms and this dynamic of protecting ourselves. We talk about past experiences and what might be helpful in creating a good learning environment and climate for our time together. We have both a profound desire to connect with other people and a deep fear of being rejected. This is in our DNA. Not long ago, if you were forced out of the herd, you would very likely perish. Launching into "course content" before addressing the interpersonal climate and our defaults that are dysfunctional for learning is folly. We always create ground rules that support the environment we wish to design. Adapting, "be nice," a favorite of one of my former students who is now a high school teacher, I like "be kind." If we can agree that we will have "no killer statements" (or gestures), we can release some of our armor and be more open for learning. Depending on the course (or other learning setting), it can be helpful to agree to confidentiality and to focus on the one person who is speaking.

My particular guidelines are less important than the rationale and spirit that guides them. An effective teacher knows and feels that teaching and learning is a shared human process. If we take for granted that we will have good connection and useful processes, we are defying what is evident about our histories as learners.

For me, much of the pleasure of teaching is in getting to know students and building relationships. I appreciate that some teachers are more engaged with the world of information and data. It may be a matter of degree how much fun you have by prioritizing people, yet it will likely yield great benefits for your teaching effectiveness if you explore human connection and build a foundation for your learning community.

4. **Always remember that you have power. Use it wisely and responsibly** – Recall Haim Ginott's comment that you are the "decisive element in the classroom." Left unchecked, your ego can play nasty tricks like that of a Little League coach. Acknowledge that you have needs and you get to be human, too. Yet, just as I have seen otherwise mentally healthy white-collar professionals act like raving lunatics at their children's sporting events, you are in a position of power and you have impact whether or not you are conscious of it. A sophisticated analysis of power (any Foucault fans out there?) is well beyond the scope of this conversation. The point here is to get clear with yourself that you have positional and systemic power. If you are a teacher who gives marks and grades, a coach who determines playing time, or a parent (in almost any situation), you have power. It can become invisible to you. Students are constantly scanning the environment and assessing if you are a threat. Although you are

unlikely to pose the physical hazard of a saber-tooth tiger, you can easily put them at mental and emotional risk.   Although some individuals, based on their personal qualities or early-career status may benefit from establishing their authority, I've found it's generally more important to diminish my clout and reduce the distance between the students and me. For sure I acknowledge the importance of establishing the "rules of engagement" and – in Joseph Campbell's terms from the hero's journey – being "the old one" and keeping the sacred place sacred. Perhaps it seems paradoxical to reduce one's perceived power while establishing that you can be counted on to "police" the environment. This is part of the challenge of finding a balance.

2 EVERYTHING I NEED TO KNOW ABOUT TEACHING I DIDN'T LEARN IN KINDERGARTEN (BUT I LEARNED A LOT IN GRADE SCHOOL)

"Look-ee Look-ee,
Don't you want a cookie?
Come on down to Room 11.
We didn't say 7 ..."

The copy may not be brilliant, but as a first foray into marketing for a group of six-year olds, it was a good start. I'm just realizing now that was a big year of contributions to my teaching wisdom. In Mrs. Weiner's first grade class, we had a bake sale where kids from the whole school came to our class. The touch of business training was a bonus. The core of the activity was experiential learning with arithmetic. We got to add up the cost of baked goods, take money, and use subtraction to make change. This was fun and real. Perhaps this planted the seeds of one of my most core beliefs about teaching and learning.

13

One of my favorite recent examples that makes the same point is this: If I asked you which do you think would have you learn more – if you had to research, design, and deliver a lecture on a topic or if you had to listen to a lecture on the same topic? I have yet to find someone who says that there would be more learning from listening than actively creating. Then how come professors get to do more learning than the students? Really. If it were not the dominant mode of so many university classes and other supposed learning situations, we might think it silly to suggest that sitting passively listening to someone else spout information would be a good way to learn. People learn by doing. It's common sense. You may have heard it said that if we learned to walk and speak in school that we would all be tripping and stuttering. Imagine trying to enable toddlers to ambulate by lecturing to them about how to walk. Maybe let them try once and give them an array of corrective feedback. Sounds goofy, doesn't it? For starters, picture children learning to walk. Notice that when they fall down they are not paralyzed by some concerns about failure. When they achieve progression toward success, they smile and are internally satisfied by achieving competence. Perhaps it is amazing that it took forty years of study and an accidental discovery for Harvard Business School professor, Teresa Amabile, to identify that the single most important factor in boosting workplace creativity, productivity, congeniality, and commitment is progress in meaningful work. We are hard-wired to increase our competence; we develop and grow through action – engaging in search strategies and adapting toward progressive success. We feel good and create a virtuous circle of continuing exploration and innovation.

Let's consider why the natural approach to learning is not so natural for teachers in formal settings. In my work with new teachers (which began observing pre-service teachers when I was a graduate research assistant), it's fairly obvious that their focus is on themselves. The worries and concerns are about what am *I* going to do? How am *I* going to look? The early phases of teaching tend to be more self-absorbed and attention is on teacher behavior. This is a perfect match for lecturing: what's my content? How will I organize it? How will I deliver it? Do I have enough to fill the time?

If one is fortunate, there is a moment of realization and a conceptual shift. I first described this as moving from "going through the motions to going after learning." In that great aha there is a profound moment that it is not about you, the teacher. The whole point is that it is about them – the students. It is less essential what *I* do and absolutely crucial to think about what they will do. Instead of preparing my actions, I begin to think about what the students will do. What is it like to be a learner in my class? How much time am I talking vs. how much time are they actively engaged in learning?

During students' small group work, I heard a skillful colleague intervene, "Please stop learning. I want to talk some more." If you accept some of the nearly self-evident premises about teaching and learning, what would you conclude if you parachuted in on a typical lecture? Gee, this person at the front of the room has done a lot of learning and is getting great practice in deepening that learning as he presents the information to these onlookers. I wonder how much he is paying them.

One of the great things about sports is that coaches are typically very invested in athletes' learning (whether their motives are healthy or not). So you almost always see learning situations (even called "practices") where there is a tremendous amount of active learning. The "students" are repeatedly attempting the behaviors directly tied to the learning outcomes. The "teachers" watch carefully, note key distinctions, offer feedback on selected attempts, provide opportunities for continued attempts, and generally improvement is evident. Although cognitive or conceptual learning may not be as clear or observable, the key factors for good teaching are consistent.

If I first got this idea in first grade, I had some marvelous reinforcement in second grade. I was blessed with another great teacher in Miss Ellen Hampton Adams. In addition to her playfulness and genuine appreciation for children, she knew something about learning by doing. We had little manila notebooks for writing whatever we wanted. I had some brilliant entries with exceptional titles like "George and I," "Tracy and I," and "Gary and I," depending on who was my "best friend" *du jour*. I recall the only instruction was to write. When we submitted the notebooks, they would come back with comments showing the teacher's interest in the story. There was no "red ink." I remember the contrast when I got my beloved writing notebook back when we had a substitute teacher and there were a bunch of corrections (in red ink). As much as I believe in the benefit of corrective feedback, there is a lot to be said about providing positive reinforcement to help a learner engage, if not love, the learning. Maybe I had a disposition or propensity for writing. (It has been suggested subsequently that I'm a sophisticated rhetorician inebriated by the exuberance of my own verbosity.) Yet, for me, it was a chance to practice a lot and to learn by doing. I believe the fact that I don't struggle with the blank page and generally like to write stems from my playful explorations in grade school.

Teaching Applications:

1. In recent years "learning outcomes" has become a "term of art." But it has probably always been implicit that a good teacher knows what a successful learner will be able to do as a result of the designed journey. "Content" is frequently the enemy of learning. It shows up in sentences like "I have too much content to cover." Learning is often compromised by "course objectives" that may describe what the teacher will do or what the course will "cover," but don't direct the students' energy and attention. Good teaching is more interested in uncovering meaning.

   Although there is a lot of vocabulary in the scholarship of teaching and learning that does more to obfuscate than elucidate (that is muddy more than clarify) what is helpful for teachers, I think "intended learning outcomes" have enormous merit. Although I imagine that a good caveman knew what he wanted his son to be able to do when he taught him to hunt, there is something to be said for explicitly stating what a successful learner will be able to do as a result of a class or course. For a detailed discussion of this topic and some great tips on what verbs to avoid and which to use, see *A Primer on Learning Outcomes* (Potter & Kustra, 2012, available at *www1.uwindsor.ca/ctl/system/files/PRIMER-on-Learning-Outcomes.pdf*)

2. Once you have the intended learning outcomes established, it will become very logical to start thinking about learning activities. What you do as a teacher is only in service of producing the desired outcomes. Unless your outcome is for students to leave your class telling their friends that you are a cornucopia of knowledge, you will probably be more circumspect about how much time you spend talking. The combination of what students do in class and what students do out of class (reading, watching videos, doing assignments) will form the majority of the learning. Think about what students will do. Consider how they will actively engage in tasks that will lead them progressively toward the learning outcomes. Become brilliant by addressing how to sequence progressive challenges and what support and guidance will assist them on their journey.

3 *A VIEW FROM THE SIDELINES*

"Billy, our coach for the under-13 boys went AWOL, do you think you could step in and coach? They have the championship game on Sunday." So began my teaching and coaching career. (I said yes.) I arrived to join a group of very well prepared boys ready for their big game. I was just a few years older than these young athletes. Mostly, I just had to manage who would start and the substitutions. It felt like fairly high stakes with a gym full of (overly) enthusiastic parents. I had certainly not yet written any kind of coaching or teaching philosophy, but my reflections show I had some foundational beliefs already in place. Of course I knew the boys and their families wanted to win and I'm sure I did, too. Yet, I was aware of having all the boys participate meaningfully and not simply keeping the most talented players on the floor. Perhaps this was the first chance for perceptions from a decade earlier to influence my approach.

The boys had organized plays and defensive

structures. Much of the important coaching had been done before I arrived. I felt what I could do was create a positive atmosphere, encourage them, and give a few tips here and there. I remember looking down the bench at some boys who were decidedly less skillful and feeling it was important to get them into the game even though the outcome was far from decided. Maybe the good fortune of the situation I fell into gave me a very positive "primacy" that helped to shape my career path. It felt really good to win the game and to get acknowledgements from parents, especially from those whose boys got more of a chance to play than might have been deemed acceptable given that this was a championship game and they were not the strongest players.

As a result of having the best record in the division, the regular coach was also in line to coach the post-season all-star game. I was offered that opportunity and gladly accepted. I got to coach a practice as well as the game. Again, I can see the roots of current beliefs in action in that first chance to run a training session. I mostly let the players play in a game situation to become familiar with each other and to have the learning match the performance situation as much as possible. I wanted it to be fun. I liked being actively involved. When it was game time, it may have been the good fortune of superior players, but I probably did some things right as we won that game, too. I recall looking across the court at the 40-something coach of the opposing team, wondering if he was irritated losing to a teenager with peach fuzz and the poor attempt of trying to look professional with a collared velour shirt.

Teaching Application

1. Teaching is full of "conflicting desiderata." You will have many moments where you have to choose between competing values. Often there will be a "crowd" (colleagues, parents, students, administrators) cheering for you to move in a particular direction. Knowing what you value most and staying true to what you believe to be most important will help you to make the best choices and will go a long way to helping you to sleep well. My research in youth sport has given much support for how espoused values like having fun and learning are challenged by external pressures (and often internal wishes) to win. As a teacher, your inner guide may direct you toward a choice or activity that will be unpopular, but ultimately will result in the best learning. In these moments, it is essential to remind your ego that you are not engaged in a popularity contest. If you are clear that optimizing students' learning and development is your "true North" it will help you navigate the tricky forks in the road.

2. Inquire about students' prior learning and observe their current capacities before falling in love with what you think you have to teach. These young basketball players were well prepared in many respects and it would have been disruptive to attempt to teach them new strategies. Establishing where your students enter your learning situation is a key task. If you assume they are ignorant of knowledge and skills that they already possess, you may

bore them and lose credibility. If you assume abilities they do not have, you may create anxiety and leave them behind. Of course, the complexity grows quickly with the typical heterogeneity of students' aptitudes. Learning how to modify instruction and learning activities for diverse students is an ongoing challenge.

4 BEST LESSONS FROM WORST MOMENTS IN COLLEGE

You've probably heard your friends or colleagues tell stories about some horrible person who they told themselves they would *never* be like. Maybe you've told such stories yourself. I remember my dad telling me that many times he was in doubt about what to do as a parent, so he would do the opposite of what he thought his father would do. Some of my greatest teaching lessons are not based on intense dislike of individuals, but on some teaching approaches that gave me a strong visceral and emotional feeling that had me recognize some things to be sure to avoid.

My least successful experience from the perspective of grades was an anatomy course I took during my last semester of my undergraduate degree. So perhaps the caveat is that this says something about misalignment for me as a learner, but I think there are some great lessons from what was a rather harsh course. The professor had been teaching medical students for a decade and this was among his first times teaching undergraduate students – and it was in the physical education curriculum. I was one of just a few students clearly interested in P.E. and I had questions about the motives of a senior biology major and psych majors who had already studied the neural anatomy (the hardest part of the course from my perspective) for taking this course. The professor was primed for the 10 a.m. bell and talked pretty close to non-stop for 50 minutes, other than the occasional question, and moved through slides like there was a prize for most clicks in a class. The exams were multiple choice with every question having four choices, followed by "E. none of the above". And we had a series of microscopes where we had to peer and identify something that was designated with an arrow, where I frequently wanted to respond, "It's purple." If this course was not 100% an exercise in memory of inert facts, I'm unclear what else was included.

Such a teaching approach may have made sense prior to the advent of the printing press. It is certainly obsolete in the age of the Internet. It was reasonable to lecture when you had the only book in town. Now that we have plentiful texts and many on-line resources, there is virtually no added value in a straight lecture. The continuing focus on information dissemination in many courses does little more than prove how slow to change we can be even when there are many better ways.

My distaste for committing little details to memory gained fuel from a basketball-coaching course that I took. One of the questions on the final exam asked for the dimensions of the court. I happened to know that it was 94 feet long, probably from a story about a fluke shot that was the length of the court. I failed to provide the correct width. That one point on the exam was apparently enough to drop my whole course grade from an A- to a B (no plus grades at Grinnell College). It was a two-credit course and it dropped by overall GPA by two-hundredths, which kept me from graduating as the student-athlete with the highest grade point average. You might conclude that I was overly invested in grades (and you might not be entirely wrong), but there is a much deeper point here.

Teaching Application:

Why do we have our students answer questions on an exam that are absolutely about recall, the lowest level of cognitive operations? Why would we not at least have students apply the information in some way or minimally call for something that involves comprehension? In the grander scheme, a big problem is that we have content-driven courses where we begin with "the stuff" or "material" we are going to teach; we design the course around chapters or topics, and then we test to see if the students can demonstrate that they crammed the information into their heads. What a magnificent waste of the possibility of having human beings gathered live together for the purpose of learning!

There are many ways to address the problem. One is a return to intended learning outcomes. If we think well about what we want students to be able to do by the end of the course, I think there are few defensible cases of it being about successful memorization. Granted there are situations where it is important to have data available for recall; for example, colleagues in pharmacy have argued vehemently for the need to memorize drug information. Yet, the extent to which we still have courses essentially following the old line about moving information from the professor's notes to the student's notes, bypassing both of their brains, is staggering and saddening. My experience is that most things that are worth memorizing happen naturally. I learn all my students' names almost instantly because it really matters to me and I see great value in doing so. I know which authors created the theories I use in my research through natural repetition. I have to ask myself if a student can find the answer on a smartphone in a matter of seconds, am I providing useful education by demanding that the fact be memorized?

It's not that memorizing *per se* is evil; it just has little value for its own sake. When information is conceptualized and connected with meaning, it tends to stick. The Heath brothers (Chip & Dan, 2007) wrote a nice book showing how teaching can have ideas adhere by using the SUCCES formula (simple, unexpected, concrete, credible, emotional, and using stories). Yes, we want important ideas to stay with students. We can help that to happen by moving from superficial information delivery to engaging students in solving real and relevant problems in a domain.

A final story that burned a pedagogical lesson into my heart happened on one of the first days of a college Spanish course. I came from an extraordinarily strong high school Spanish education: during my senior year I attended an alternative program that was part of the public high school in which we were on trimesters with longer class sessions, every other day.

The first trimester there were three of us, the second there were two, and the final was a one-on-one with the teacher and me. I also had reinforcement from playing soccer with friends from Venezuela and Spain, giving me lots of real world practice. I entered my college Spanish with advance placement credit and I was confident and ready to go. The instructor asked a question: "¿Que es un héroe?" ("what is a hero?") Are you kidding me, right in my wheelhouse – I had studied El Cid and was rooted in Joseph Campbell's hero's journey. I raised my hand and responded proudly when called upon. I described the hero as the central character, the protagonist, and offered some substance on the typical path of the hero. The teacher responded, "umm," coupled with a dismissive face and searched for the answer she was looking for. The substantial wind was completely obliterated from my sail. I didn't last long in her class.

Teaching Application:

Recall that every student arrives in your class with a history of moments like these and usually ones that are much worse or at least happened at younger, more vulnerable ages. It is a risk for a student to participate in your class. It takes courage to engage. It often takes overcoming an intelligent part of the student's system that says, "Remember when you raised your hand before and it didn't work out – don't do it." If you don't want to spend weeks asking questions and watching your students getting very interested in the intricacies of the hues and patterns on their desks, you want to get this point. Do what you can to provide encouragement, appreciation, and acknowledgment every time that a student participates. I'm not saying you should applaud the content of a response that is off target. I'm suggesting that you honor the person and the act of participating.

I also recommend that you give up a questioning technique that I call "fishing." When there is only one correct answer, when there is only one accurate factual response, you may do well to reconsider asking the question. (There's a scene from *Ferris Bueller* ... "Anyone? Anyone? Bueller?" that makes this point painfully clear.) I've seen this procedure used even in doctoral courses, "Does anyone recall who created social facilitation theory?" Consider the options: one or more students know the correct answer ... they have to decide if it is worth it to reply ... if it seems obvious, they risk being the teacher's pet (or your favorite disparaging term); they may pause and see if anyone else answers ... it may get so uncomfortable waiting that they give the correct response. What was gained? Or imagine that someone provides an answer that was not what you were looking for ... you just have to let them know that they are wrong. What's the benefit here? Or no one knows or no one will volunteer an answer ... you are forced to give the answer to your own question. Was there some thoughtful reflection? Nope – just recall it successfully, never knew it, or get it wrong.

Good, useful questions go beyond recall. Whether in class or on an exam, questions should challenge students to apply, synthesize, think critically and creatively. A great classroom atmosphere is abuzz with student participation. Part of that is based on creating a sufficiently safe environment. It is maintained and bolstered by positive support for participation. Great teachers seem to have an ability to turn every response into a contribution.

I have learned to respect and dignify the vulnerability of students' participation and engagement. I am truly grateful to students who share their thoughts and feelings.

5 *NOTHING LIKE CAMP*

Check out Google images for "camp counselor." You will see a lot of smiling faces, often surrounded by many smiling children. In the same way that some people will tell you that the best thing you can do in life is to get a dog, or go on a meditation retreat, or try bungee jumping, I will suggest that one of the best things an aspiring teacher can do is to work at a summer camp. I spent most of my summers during my post-secondary education as a camp counselor. In addition to having a great time and making lifelong friends, I had many tremendous experiences that helped me to develop as a teacher. There were lots of low stakes opportunities to try out teaching, leadership, and presenting techniques and approaches with willing participants.

During one of my first orientations, we had one of the best presenters I've seen in any venue, Michael Brandwein. Among his lessons was "if you're not making it fun, you're doing it wrong." Some would argue whether that holds true for a camp counselor. I imagine many would say that's not a useful suggestion for teachers in formal academic settings. I say it's worthy of consideration. Not everything is going to be fun (at least not for everybody), but what if you tried to bring some fun and playfulness to everything you did? There were things I considered, but decided against – like wondering how to make the requisite nail cutting fun for 12 year-old boys ... perhaps see how big a pile of clippings we could collect ... conclusion: too gross. Yet many other things from getting the boys up in the morning to making beds and cleaning the cabin to coming together and winding down for sleeping at the end of the day were all moments that could have been mundane or unpleasant that we managed to make fun. I've subsequently studied enough about laughter, humour, and positive psychology to make a strong case for why fun enhances learning. In short, if all the negative experiences discussed earlier can close people down for learning, fun and the power of play open people up to explore, innovate, and learn.

Camp also gave me some of my first chances to be in front of an audience beyond my childhood acting experiences. I discovered the pleasure of performing and how elements of theatre or acting could be highly useful in grabbing attention, engaging learners, and making ideas memorable. There was another great example here from Michael Brandwein. He did a magic trick that involved passing a needle through a balloon. As he was talking, he would move the pointy end of the needle toward the balloon and the audience would cringe in anticipation of a big pop. He certainly kept us with him through this technique. (The climax of the trick was passing the needle through the balloon without it popping. Over twenty years after seeing him perform, I learned the trick and have used it in workshops as a marvelous example of perspectives, assumptions, and what is possible.)

Another of his lessons is far more useful to me when working with elementary students than undergrads, but the core idea may be broadly applicable (even in relationships with colleagues and friends). He shared a story of a child who would resort to crying to get what she wanted. The child had learned at home that breaking down into tears was an effective way to produce desired outcomes. He used some plastic baby toy of keys on a key ring to offer the idea that if you want to take one key away, you need to provide another one. If the key works for the kid, why would they be willing to relinquish it unless they have another way to get what they want? The following autumn, when I was monitoring recess during my elementary school teaching practicum, a little girl came up to me, clearly upset and asking for my help. Through tears and whining, she was trying to convey what she wanted from me. Almost exactly like Mr. Brandwein's demonstration, I said to her, "I would really like to help you, but I can't understand what you are saying. Can you please tell me what you want so I can hear you?" Seemingly as magical as the needle going through the balloon, her crying stopped instantly, her speaking got clear, and in a totally audible and comprehensible fashion, she told me how I could help her.

Teaching Applications:
Some of the points here are probably obvious.

Any time you can add play and fun to a class, it will make it more engaging; and as many proponents of good teaching methods suggest, using elements of dramatic skills can enhance your teaching. The "key exchange" method may merit further explication. Consider all the various things your students do that were useful ways to get what they wanted at an earlier stage in their life that are no longer optimal (you may also notice that you have a considerable set of such behaviors yourself). Before you ask students to stop such a behavior, you may find it quite productive to consider how they perceive this action or way of being is working for them. For example, I've run across many students who believe that "pulling an all-nighter" or cramming at the last minute is the only way to prepare for an exam. Whether their methods for concluding that this approach is valuable is sound or not, they may cling to it. Before they will consider giving up this "key," you will do well to offer a convincing case and a path to follow for studying in a progressive way over time.

6 LESSONS FROM GRADUATE SCHOOL

Sometimes you actually learn something while you are in school. Often the best things are not necessarily what was intended in the curriculum. Graduate school inadvertently taught me a lot about the structure of education and provided me with my first opportunities to teach undergraduate classes.

My father, who was a professor of social work, noted that often students in training seemed to be more effective with certain kinds of patients than were their professional counterparts, most likely because of their degree of empathy. Perhaps because I was just barely removed from being an undergraduate student myself, I think I was well positioned to relate to students. My first classes were in the physical activity program at the University of Iowa, and were offered pass/fail. This context helped to facilitate somewhat more comfortable and informal relationships than other settings. I enjoyed my new role and it helped to lay the foundation for my teaching approaches.

Although my Masters thesis was about the business and educational models of intercollegiate athletics, in many ways the underlying concern went back to Little League and the importance of student/athlete centeredness. My academic research deepened my understanding and my resolve about human connection. By interviewing student-athletes participating in divergent programs, I saw how the coaches' and the institutions' approach influenced the degree of humanity and concern for the whole person.

My doctoral research, although I don't think I was remotely aware of it at the time, was the fruition of exploring the questions raised when I was six years-old relative to what coaches and parents believe (they are teachers) and how systems can be designed to take care of participants, or not. In retrospect, I can see I was seeking answers about the quagmire that I witnessed in my nascent years. Part of what my studies revealed suggested that it is probably much more difficult to educate and change individuals than it is to alter the environment. For example, getting all coaches to see the merits of giving each young athlete the same opportunities to learn and to perform may be much more challenging than having a league implement an equal playing time rule. There are probably many elements of educational contexts that follow this principle. Think about the ways in which the structures you work in direct you to organize and evaluate in particular manners. Consider how different rules and regulations would foster different outcomes. To paraphrase Marx, we have choices about how we teach, but often not in the situations of our choosing. (To paraphrase the other Marx, I wouldn't want to work at a school that would have me as a teacher.)

Also during my time at the University of Illinois, I worked as a research assistant for a professor who studied pre-service teachers. I got to go out and observe and interview undergraduate students who were preparing to become physical education teachers. This was a rich experience that illustrated more about contextual limitations as well as the developmental process for new teachers. In a very general sense, it seems like almost all new teachers have their attention on themselves. This is a very natural and human response to the concerns about looking good and avoiding looking bad, as well as all of our other worries, such as will I have enough content and activities to fill the allotted time. It was also easy to notice that new teachers were following various implicit scripts or were "going through the motions." The greatest insight from these investigations was that there was a key moment of conceptual shift – as if it dawned on the developing educators the great value in paying attention to the students, becoming curious about what it was like to be in their classes. I described this as shifting from going through the motions to "going after learning." I had my own version of that transition during this time.

I did my first undergraduate lectures to large classes and I began to develop some elements of showmanship. I also recall moving beyond preparing my lecture content to thinking about what kinds of engaging experiences I could create to foster students' learning. One of my earliest adventures was for a class about reinforcement theory. As students gave correct answers, I gave them candy. I purposely went back to a student who had a treat and asked a challenging question; when the student gave a wrong answer, I took away the candy – demonstrating both positive reinforcement and punishment. It was trickier to have them experience negative reinforcement (when a response or behavior is strengthened by stopping, removing or avoiding a negative outcome or aversive stimulus), which is often confused with punishment. One way was to have students make annoying sounds around a student until a correct answer was given. I thought it was a good and fun way to get at the concepts, but my point was that I had moved my focus from what I was doing to what the students would experience to promote their own learning.

Teaching Applications

1. For sure we all bring personal foibles to our teaching. It is absolutely human to want to look good, to be liked, and to feel competent. To some extent, these concerns never go away. If we can accept our humanity and bring some lightness to it, our focus can shift away from our selves. Part of how I look at it is that it is a welcome relief from self-absorption to get my attention off myself and on to the students. It is actually a lot more fun and freeing to concentrate on the students and to be keenly engaged with their learning than it is to worry about my ego. It should seem beyond obvious that teaching is about the students. Unfortunately so many aspects of education and what goes

on in classes appear to be more in service of the teacher than students' learning. Consider where you can shift your focus from what you will do as a teacher to what your students will do to facilitate their learning.

2. Experts seem to concur that elements of good teaching involve some performance and entertainment. I've had ardent colleagues argue that it is not their job to entertain. Well … if you are in front of the room and want people to pay attention, wouldn't it be good to earn it? I think there's a useful distinction that is easily missed here. The intended outcomes are still about learning; you are not trying to create a satisfied audience for the sake of entertainment. The point is to use methods and approaches *in service* of facilitating learning. Some of us are more theatrical and enjoy the performative elements more than others. Yet I've seen more reserved instructors brilliantly implement drama that does not require them to be brilliant thespians. The place to look is student engagement. Whereas you may need to step out of your comfort zone, you also want to select techniques that are a match for your style. Generally I find students are an appreciative audience and the fact that you are trying may be what is most important. One of my favorite memories involves co-teaching with a senior colleague during my first

year at University of Alberta. When the distinguished, gray-bearded professor joined me in a rap, let's be sure Eminem had nothing to worry about, but the students went wild.

7 "WE WANT TO NOMINATE YOU": THE GENESIS OF EXHILARATED LEARNING

It was the greatest misrepresentation by a pronoun in my life. A member of my University's administration approached me with the statement, "**We** want to nominate you for the 3M National Teaching Fellowship." I was extremely honoured and, quite frankly, it had taken multiple requests over a number of years before I was open to being considered (recall our deepest fear). The nomination required a 50-page dossier and the vast majority of it became my task. Although some elements called for gathering of data like student ratings of instruction, much of it called for reflection on questions that I had never adequately considered. When asked to provide the underpinnings of my teaching and the practices that demonstrated my beliefs and my effectiveness, I had to excavate in places I had not pondered. It ended up being one of the most interesting and useful reflective exercises I've undertaken and it culminated in three foundational dimensions of what I've come to call "Exhilarated Learning" (Strean, 2012). Here's how I described it, which will recall some themes explored above.

Human connection: The first dimension

In virtually any learning environment, students enter with some level of tension, anxiety, and/or resistance. If the stress response is activated, it can decrease the brain's capabilities to learn and remember (Kaufeldt, 2010). University students have witnessed classrooms for at least a dozen years in which students can be humiliated, put down, or made wrong. At a very basic level, students entering a classroom are asking, "does the professor mean me any harm?" When the instructor creates a welcoming environment and develops positive relationships with students, it puts students more at ease and facilitates learning. One of the most fundamental principles in effective teaching is increasing teacher/student contact and connection (Chickering & Gamson, 1987; Lowman, 1995).

Largely under-emphasized in traditional teaching skills programs, this dimension acts on the inevitable wall and unwritten contract between teacher and students. On the students' side, it creates comfort and it predisposes learners to explore the content and to remain open to the possibility of suggested behavioural or conceptual changes. On the instructor's side, it may enhance the teacher's confidence, awareness, presence, authenticity, and commitment to results. Many classroom practices such as establishing ground rules, using icebreaker activities, and facilitating relationships between and among students can contribute to a sense of human connection and enhance learning.

Whole-body engagement: The second dimension

University education is often characterized as an experience that occurs above the neck. Stereotypes include passing information from the notes of the professor to the notes of the student, bypassing both of their minds. Most of our understanding of the mind and rationality are based on metaphors that are not supported by cognitive science. Take for example the enduring notion that rational thought is dispassionate. We know this to be false from studies in neuroscience (Damasio, 1994). Those who have lost the capacity to be emotionally engaged in their lives cannot reason appropriately about moral issues. The traditional Western conception of the person with disembodied reason and an objective world must be replaced with the conception of an embodied person. Among the important implications for teaching and learning is the recognition of the centrality of emotion. All learning occurs in a mood and part of fostering student engagement includes attending to and managing the mood of the classroom.

Including emotions, moods, and the importance of the whole body is a completely different paradigm from simple learning styles (for a thorough critique of "learning styles," see Strean, 2016). Whole-body engagement leverages all thinking-feeling-acting channels that people use to absorb new information, concepts, and skills. Students become significantly more engaged with the experiential methods encompassed in this dimension. This may promote faster transfer of knowledge and skills and higher retention rates (e. g., Barnes, 2005). This dimension goes beyond adding to the typical information dissemination mode; it re-conceptualizes the learner and the learning process.

Content to context: The third dimension

One of the biggest challenges for instructors is to keep the parts connected to the whole. This component is all about the importance of a big picture focus. Particularly in the delivery of a semester-long course, it is increasingly challenging and important to connect the pieces to the larger pie. Much of education, training, and courseware design historically have been linear and reductionist, which often leaves learners lost and with no overarching vision of the learning objective or purpose of segmented activities. This dimension brings in one of the most essential, but often forgotten, elements of successful education. Learners need to have the parts connected to the whole (Meron & Peled, 2004). Teachers need to be mindful of learners' developing schemata and draw connections among new information and concepts and learners' prior knowledge (e.g., Zheng, Yang, Garcia, & McCaddens, 2008). Building the connections among bits of content and the broader context provides scaffolding for incorporating new information, facilitates a learner's ability to decide where to pay close attention, helps make inferences, provides a guide to search for memory, aids in editing and summarizing, and helps produce hypotheses about information that is missing (cf. Anderson & Pichert, 1978).

Teachers facilitate learning by offering practical

44

strategies for students to develop schemata when reading, listening to a lecture, or otherwise being exposed to new ideas such that students are able to recognize familiar ideas and make connections to the text or new ideas. With enough practice, modeling, and exposure, teachers can implement some of these strategies in their classrooms to accommodate students (Navarro, 2008). Awareness of the constant interplay between specific content and the larger context provides students with both the why and the how that will produce with deeper, more meaningful learning and greater satisfaction.

These three dimensions capture much of what I've shared in my personal journey and my hope is that you have found ideas and practices that will support you in providing Exhilarated Learning for your students. (Another essential factor in your ability to do so is your own ALIVEness, which you can learn how to foster in with the assistance of my forthcoming book. The following three bonus chapters give you a taste of what's coming.)

References

Anderson, R. C., & Pichert, J. W. (1978). Recall of previously unrecallable information following a shift in perspective. *Journal of Verbal Learning and Verbal Behavior, 17*, 1-12.

Barnes, J. (2005). "You could see it on their faces . . . " The importance of provoking smiles in schools. *Health Education, 105*(5), 392-400

Chickering, A. W., & Gamson, Z. F. (1987). Seven principles for good practice in undergraduate education. *AAHE Bulletin*, 3-7.

Damasio A. R. (1994). *Descartes' error: Emotion, reason and the human brain*. New York: Grosset/Putnam.

Kaufeldt, M. (2010). *Begin with the brain: Orchestrating the learner-centered classroom*. Thousand Oaks, CA: Corwin.

Lowman, J. (1995). *Mastering the techniques of teaching* (2nd ed.). San Francisco: Jossey-Bass.

Meron, R., & Peled, I. (2004). Situated or abstract: The effect of combining context and structure on constructing an additive (part–part–whole) schema. Bergen, Norway: *International Group for the Psychology of Mathematics Education*.

Navarro, A. (2008). Building schema for English language learners. (ERIC Document Reproduction Service No. ED514335). Retrieved August 18, 2011 from EBSCOHost ERIC database.

Strean, W. B. (2012). Exhilarated learning and the scholarship of engagement: From here (the university) to the horizon (the community). *Collected Essays on Learning and Teaching, 5*, 179-183.

Strean, W. B. (2016). Do yogis have "learning

styles"? *International Journal of Yoga, 10*(1), 37-39.

Zheng, R.Z., Yang, W., Garcia, D., & McCadden, E. P. (2008). Effects of multimedia and schema induced analogical reasoning on science learning. *Journal of Computer Assisted Learning, 24,* 474–482. doi: 10.1111/j.1365-2729.2008.00282.x

An embodied path to joy and harmony

Bonus Chapter 1
COME ALIVE!:
*INTRODUCTION TO A MODEL FOR
EXHILARATED TEACHING*

"You are enough. Be more." — Billy Strean

Even if you are thoroughly convinced that all the ideas in Part I are brilliant and you are totally enrolled in applying the teaching approaches that I advocated, it will be spectacularly difficult to follow through unless you are taking good care of your self. To paraphrase a good line from a first date, "Enough about teaching, let's talk about you."

Our internal monologues are filled with phrases like, "I'm not good enough," "I'm not worthy," and "I'm not lovable." Countless books and interventions speak to that broken part of you and seek to offer you as simple a solution as possible to shut those voices up. Let's examine another path. Let's begin with the premise that although we could always find problems or shortcomings, it's a lot more fun and a lot more productive to wake up by focusing on the positive. In fact, neuroscience and positive psychology are showing us that when we try to push away the negative, we actually engage and activate the negative. Trying not to be anxious or angry is not going to work. We've got to activate the positive. We can also embrace the challenging and complex journey that combines several dimensions at the level of self, other, and nature.

I love to cook. Following a recipe can produce a wonderful outcome that creates satisfaction and pleasure. Perhaps we are seeking a similar recipe for life. In some sense, I am hoping to provide such a recipe. Yet, what I believe makes a joyful, fully alive existence so challenging is that most aspects of life that matter involve constant balance and integration. There is yin and yang in everything. We must always be in questions of how much is too much and how much is too little. This is complicated by the fact that the elusive sweet spot is dynamic. Each relationship requires feeling into what produces a sense of distance and what results in a sense of invasion. The amount that works in one moment will be different from what works in another. There is a story involving a famous sitar player who wanted to study meditation asking the Buddha "Should I control my mind or should I completely let go?" The Buddha queried how the great musician would tune the strings of his instrument. The musician responded that he would make them not too tight and not too loose. The Buddha posed that in meditation practice you should not impose anything too forcefully on the mind, nor should you let it wander. The way of letting the mind be in a very open way, of feeling the flow of energy without trying to subdue it and without letting it run out of control, of going with the energy pattern of mind is the meditation practice.

In finding the many points and moments of balance, the foundation is awareness. We cultivate awareness through mindfulness and build our capacities to sense and feel the many and varied dynamic solutions to how much is just right. You may not have realized that the secret to life was right there in *Goldilocks*.

Most of the ways in which people pursue "the good life" strike me as having an ironic seriousness. There is often a mood of struggle or forceful persistence. The path of aliveness that we are exploring here seeks to be a joyful journey. With a mood of curiosity, openness, and play, we embark on an exploration of five foundational (fun-dational?) factors that contribute to living an exhilarated life. There is a good reason why you so frequently hear Gandhi's quotation, "Be the change you wish to see in the world;" it makes so much sense. If you want to have a lively and engaging classroom, you must be the energy you wish to see in the room.

From this background of awareness and attention, the ALIVE model builds the foundation with all the things that almost everyone knows, but almost no one does: getting enough sleep and recovery, drinking enough water, eating good food, and getting enough physical activity. This combines for A = Attention and energy.

L = Loving relationships is the second

dimension and will explore all of our communication, connection, caring, and kindness that is so crucial for our well-being and joy.

I = Inspired passion and purpose is the third component may be like the cutting edge of the factors that drive us toward what we care about. Here you'll see how to find your deepest connection to what you care about and progressively align yourself to how you can express your creativity and serve the world.

V= Ventures into nature is the fourth element where you will re-connect to with planet and find rich sources of energy, peace, and wellbeing.

E = Enjoyment and is the mood for the path to ALIVEness. One of the secrets you'll find here is in experiencing your full emotional range and the power of placing your non-judgmental awareness on what you're feeling.

Although we can consider the five parts in turn, there is a synergy in which all are pieces of a whole that will serve you on the path to be fully energized, awake, and exhilarated.

Bonus Chapter 2

PRIMAL FEELINGS:
UNDERSTANDING THE SYNERGY OF SELF, OTHERS, AND NATURE

Dennis was a classic seeker. His bookshelves were lined with tomes on diet, exercise, spirituality, alternative health, creativity, better sex, secrets of relationships, happiness, and how to be your own best friend. With a near photographic memory, Dennis *knew* more about these subjects than several gurus have forgotten. Yet, little had changed in his life, despite his vast grasp of information. He had bought into the widely accepted idea that by gathering knowledge, thinking and analyzing, we will change. Dennis also took on all of these topics in isolation and failed to benefit from the great synergies and necessary connections among physical, emotional, relational, and natural wellness.

How you are like an elephant and a rider (and how to motivate the elephant)

Imagine that you are the rider, sitting on top of an elephant. Look to your right and consider that you want to get to the closest wall (or move 25 feet). But the elephant under you is thinking, "Not so much, I like it here." My money is on the elephant. You represent your higher order thinking and your powerful analytic mind. The elephant is everything else – your emotions and your basic biology. Your life has been full of examples of people trying to get you to change by giving you more information. Think of all the failed public health campaigns that were predicated on getting the latest studies into people's hands with the notion that the data would make people make better choices. The rider may be convinced, but that's not going to do you much good in changing the course of action. It's now time to reveal what the top change experts advocate: when we see something that has us *feel* something, then we change. As you consider what you have "learned" thus far and the path ahead, continue to remind yourself that knowing is the booby prize. With each possible opportunity for more energy, better relationships, greater purpose, more connection, and more fun, tap into the feeling you have and the emotion you will create. That will drive you forward.

"People rely on intelligence to solve problems, and they are naturally baffled when comprehension proves impotent to effect emotional change. To the neocortical brain, rich in the power of abstractions, understanding makes all the difference, but it doesn't count for much in the neural systems that evolved before understanding existed. Ideas bounce like so many peas off the sturdy incomprehension of the limbic and reptilian brains. The dogged implicitness of emotional knowledge, its relentless unreasoning force, prevents logic from granting salvation just as it precludes self-help books from helping. The sheer volume and variety of self-help paraphernalia testify at once to the vastness of the appetite they address and their inability to satisfy it" (Lewis, Amini, & Lannon, 2000, p. 118).

If you are not convinced that your mammalian and reptilian brains will win the battle with your cerebral cortex, ponder this example: Have you ever been having a heated conversation, perhaps with your spouse or person very close to you, and you hear yourself say something and the "smart part" of your brain comments to you "OH, that was bad, I'm going to be in big trouble for that?" But then you notice that your mouth keeps moving? Once your amygdala has dumped the chemicals, it takes a Herculean effort to override it by using your logic. Just take a look around; if we were a world of rational, information processors, would anyone start smoking?

Separation and Connection

Let's couple this idea with another disturbing illusion: our view of being individuals separate from others and from nature. To our personal and collective peril, we operate largely like we are disconnected from ourselves, each other, and our planet. Each of these disconnections creates profound problems. As a result of not feeling our sensations and emotions and not accessing the wisdom of the body, we are walking around tired, thirsty, hungry, out of shape, and distracted. We are facing unprecedented levels of self-inflicted disease, diminished performance, and discontent. Our lack of feeling ourselves makes it difficult to "feel into" others and perceive their concerns and yearnings. Our disconnection from others allows any kind of conflict to escalate more quickly to aggression and violence. Our lack of relationship with nature allows us to soil and rape the planet. These disconnections exacerbate our problems; working with the synergies dramatically facilitates our solutions.

The notion that we are all connected goes

beyond a new age platitude; it is a scientific reality. At a deeper level, we can imagine that each person is like a cell in a body; we are collaborating toward collective health or we are heading off in our own direction, like a cancer.

It would be great if our problems could be solved with a one-dimensional approach. The challenge is more significant and the solution is more multi-faceted.

Many approaches address only one element of the difficulties we face. Whether it is mindfulness, diet, communication, or a wilderness expedition, no matter how effective the intervention, it is like providing one leg of a four-legged stool – the foundation and sustainability are lacking.

The ALIVE model offers practical methods to re-connect to self, others, and the planet. We can begin my recognizing that we have grown up with a false bill of goods that taught us that the mind is separate from the body. If we function like a computer, we don't need to take care of our whole self while our cognition churns away. Wellness and aliveness grow from experiencing the synergy of thinking, feeling and acting. This view allows us to build a foundation of practical wisdom, grounded compassion, and skillful action (Strozzi-Heckler, 2007).

Caring for your self is social

One of the most common reasons why people don't do all the things that will promote their own wellbeing is that they feel selfish. You probably know people (maybe you) who will easily drop what they are doing to do a favor or take care of a child or a friend, but won't carve out the time to do what would help them to flourish. Let's toss out those bad ideas and construct a more accurate and satisfying view: your investment in your own flourishing and thriving may be your greatest social contribution. Isn't it self-evident that if you are tired, uninspired, and unwell that you are less pleasant to be around and you probably bring others down – and if you are energized, upbeat, and vibrant, you have a positive influence on the people you meet?

As Tone-Loc (1989) said, "Let's do it."

References

Lewis T., Amini F., & Lannon R. (2000). *A general theory of love*. New York: Random House.

Strozzi-Heckler, R. (2007). Leadership dojo. In P. Holman, T. Devane, & S. Cady (Eds.), *The changehandbook* (2nd ed., pp. 239–243). San Francisco: Berrett-Koehler.

Bonus Chapter 3

[This Chapter will follow the chapters that go through each of the factors of the ALIVE model in *ALIVE!: An embodied path to joy and harmony.*
You can use it to help you to implement your teaching goals based on the suggested teaching applications above.]

ACTIONS:
TURNING GOOD IDEAS INTO YOUR WAY OF BEING

"We can't achieve what we truly desire in our heart of hearts if we don't take daily action in support of our intentions. … It is not a form of self control as much as determination to take action based upon what we truly want in this life"

— Chögyam Trungpa

"Insights are like flatulence." – Billy Strean (Zero Google results for this quotation)

Doesn't everybody love a good insight? Don't you adore a good idea? Don't you feel good about yourself whenever you finish a book like this? Don't you feel like crap a week or two later when you realize you haven't implemented any of the good ideas? The good news about a fart is that you can't hang on to it and no matter how bad it is, it will fade away fairly quickly. The bad news about insights and good ideas is that you can't hang onto them and no matter how wonderful they are, they will fade away fairly quickly.

The difference between mediocrity and thriving is largely about turning insights and good ideas into persistent action. It is our practices that shift who we are and that provide us with our results. Although we could spend our lives analysing our inaction, the more we can "just do it" as we unravel our challenges, the more effective we tend to be. One of the best ways to move to action is through goal setting. Unfortunately, much of what is often espoused and used for setting goals is not optimal. Unless you have been camping under a large stone for an extended period, you have encountered "SMART goals." The way people present these ideas is like they should be etched into stone tablets. The evidence says otherwise; one study found only 25% of people are motivated by SMART goals and for the rest, they increase stress while reducing motivation, creativity, and resilience (McKee, 1991). Another study proposed SMART goals dull responsiveness to the complex and emergent nature of organizational life (Weick & Sutcliffe, 2007). There are three ways in which your goal setting can be revolutionized: priming motivation, including AMP factors, and setting MTO goals. [These are also wonderful ways to set goals with your students.]

Priming Motivation[1]

Jumping into goals without considering priming motivation is like heading out on a road trip without filling your gas tank. One of the major ways to stimulate your motivation is to recognize your strengths and connect them with your goals. People who get to use their strengths regularly at work tend to stay at their jobs, have more productive business units, and create greater customer satisfaction. This can hold true for you at work and with other goals. The VIA Strengths Survey (http://www.viacharacter.org/) is one of the most reliable and valid tools in social science that can help you to identify your character strengths (it is a snap shot: my top five over the past seven years have consistently included Creativity, Gratitude, & Perseverance; most recently Perspective & Kindness showed up; previously Bravery and Valor & Humor and Playfulness made it; you can see how connecting with these strengths could fuel me before embarking on this book writing goal).

It also will tend to make you more optimistic, persistent, courageous, and resilient in pursuing your goals if you acknowledge your prior progress and successes. Think about when you have attempted a new challenge and you were able to see similarity to hurdles you have cleared previously. It built your confidence and gave you energy to move toward your goal. So before you follow the brilliant ideas below, spend some time writing your accomplishments, strengths, and progress that will provide fodder before you take action.

AMP Goals: [1] Taking it to another level

Whereas SMART goals have some serious shortcomings, you will see how adding Alignment, Mastery, and Pathways will serve your goal attainment. (Some of these concepts fit more with organizational goals, but you can adapt to your personal goals where need be.) To begin, you are never striving in isolation. In many work contexts, you can see how Alignment with corporate or department goals is essential for performance goal setting. Yet, if you consider the personal goals you will set in line with the ALIVE model, you can see that how they align with your family and/or other social contexts will be significant. Next, a way to take the stress out of goals and embellish them with excitement is to link them with your basic drive for learning and growth –the Mastery factor. Especially at work, and even more so when goals are set with a supervisor, it can feel like the goals are good for the institution, but it may be unclear what you get out of it. If you address the key skills and competencies you will build through your goals and, perhaps how they fit with your career aspirations, you own the goals to a greater extent and you are more galvanized to pursue them. My favourite component of this model is the Pathways to be considered for goals. It borders on ridiculous to set goals without getting specific about how you will fulfill them. If we were going to meet somewhere later today and you knew you only had enough time to get there without trial and error and all you had was the destination (address), what would you do? You probably wouldn't think twice before

62

using your map app to get directions. This may seem really simple, but it is a part of the secret sauce of goal setting. Why do so many New Years resolutions fall flat? Among the key reasons is they are expressed as wishes, like "I would like to lose 20 pounds." You might even have a date by when you hope to achieve the result, write it down, and post it on your wall. A very SMART goal, but without a Pathway, it will be like little more than buying a lottery ticket. If you got precise about how you would change your eating and exercise behaviours, so you had as clear a map as your driving directions, your likelihood of success shoots up dramatically.

MTO Goals[2]

If I like Pathways, I absolutely love this idea of how to alter people's fundamental experience of goal setting. When we look at how people are disposed to set goals – and I say this both from the literature and vast experience with individuals as a sport psychologist and coach – they tend to set goals that are too high or too low. These are both ways of saving face. People will set goals that are not challenging and they achieve them, avoiding looking bad, but they have little impact. Even worse, is when goals are so hard that although no one really expects you to achieve them – again allowing you to avoid looking really bad – they have even less impact on motivation than the easy-peasy goals. The way you beat these very common problems is ... drum roll ... set three goals. Yes, for whatever you want to do be it lose weight, run longer, make more money, learn a new skill, or obtain more clients, you set three goals. If you lean toward having your goals too low, we might say you set Minimum goals; ones you pretty much know you can achieve. If you err toward saying you will run a marathon when you've never trotted around your block, you tend toward Outrageous goals. The kind of goal that is at least a bit of a stretch, but seems attainable, we call a Target goal. Now here's the magic of setting all three. You have the Minimum goal to comfort your fear of failure. You pretty much know you've got it and you can have some success if you make it. You have the Target goal to pull you forward to a greater extent. If you under-estimated and hit the Target too quickly or easily, you have a bigger stretch of an Outrageous goal. I have seen this work so well across ages, gender, and contexts – from young elite female gymnasts to grey-haired CEOs. When I work with entrepreneurs, the MTO goals work beautifully to get them moving toward business milestones. MTO goals are great when envisioning how quickly you wish to reach a benchmark. Once you've tried it, yourself and/or with your kids or clients, you will never want to set a single goal again. It will be lonely without its two friends.

Progress

Once you have set goals in this desirable way, you may find that so much of your continuing creativity, productivity, congeniality, and commitment will be based on making strides in meaningful work. Teresa Amabile (2011) expressed this as the single most important factor for these measures in *The Progress Principle*. Just as you will want to have your catchphrase and movements to lock in happiness, it is important to celebrate your small wins, breakthroughs, and forward movement as you learn from failure and see your positive impact on others. The clichés about life being a journey and not a destination are all apropos here.

Failure

One way of simplifying why MTO goals work is that they dramatically reduce the likelihood of failure. Sometimes people avoid setting goals because they create a reality and an accountability at which they can fail. There are great clichés here, too, like failure to plan is planning to fail. But if you don't create any goals, you can kid yourself into thinking that you are doing fine or you are not failing. But why is failure such a nasty thing that it would keep us from moving forward on many of the things we care about. Let's take a deep dive into failure and possibly shift your [and your students'] relationship with failure.

"Failure is an event. It's not a person." – Zig Ziglar

If you have ever heard the popular motivational speaker from Alabama, you can hear his loud and enthusiastic drawl punching out these words. He nailed it. If failure is not personal, if it is something that happens, it is far easier to cope with. If you relate to not achieving a goal as "I failed" and quickly morph that into "I am a failure," now you have a big drama to overcome. If failure is simply something that happens, it can be an opportunity to learn about what could be added to who you were being and/or what you were doing so that you can reach your goal. You can see where there are new actions to take or a different way to take them. Failure begins to loosen its grab.

"Fail faster to succeed sooner" - David Kelly, the CEO of IDEO, one of the world's most innovative companies

There is real brilliance in this statement. For most skills, there are a somewhat predictable number of errors you will make on the path to competence. Think about learning to ride a bike. You will tip to the left, you will tip to the right, and you will stall out. If you were to avoid experiencing the places that didn't work, it would prolong the time it took you to be riding. If you tell yourself that any learning will require some discomfort, unfamiliarity, and moments of incompetence, it can be like pulling off a bandage all at once to try to experience these moments as quickly as possible. It is hilarious that we will attempt something we've never done before and want to do it right the first time. If we began with curiosity and actively sought out the errors that would lead us to successful performance, we would avoid the suffering and become competent with greater speed.

"Only those who are asleep make no mistakes." - Ingvar Kamprad, founder of IKEA, world's largest furniture brand

This comment acknowledges that if we are human and taking action in the world, we are going to make mistakes. Rather than wrestling with reality and being upset that we are doing so, we can embrace our foibles and imperfections. If we accept that we will make wrong turns and have utter fiascos, we can keep striving more easily. If we relate to bumps in the road as colossal problems that require a big emotional response before continuing, we will have slow and painful progress.

"If you don't make mistakes, you're not working on hard enough problems. And that's a big mistake." - Frank Wilczek, 2004 Nobel Prize winner in physics

I am increasingly convinced that much of our ennui and ineffectiveness comes from not having big enough problems. When I catch myself being worried or upset about what other people are doing or what evaluators think of little old me, it's evidence that I am not on purpose. This quotation also reminds me of when I taught waterskiing at summer camp. If kids would make it around a loop of the lake without falling, they most likely were not learning. If we take on worthwhile challenges, we are going to make mistakes, encounter rejection, and spend some time scratching our heads wondering what to do next. This can be good news. If everything is coming easy, you are heading toward the boredom side of Flow and you may get stale. ALIVEness happens when you are pursuing stretch goals.

"A man's errors are his portals of discovery." – James Joyce

So are a woman's and if you are starting to feel like I'm beating a lifeless horse, it's because I know that this topic is worth the emphasis. A powerful relationship with "failure" is one of the best ways to forward the time you spend in that sweet spot of great experience and great performance. A true commitment to learning and continuous improvement means welcoming errors as pathways to new understanding. Think about how much Thomas Edison absorbed on his way to creating the electric light.

"What is the best mistake you ever made?"- asked in a 21-day Gratitude Challenge.

When you ponder all of these quotations and perspectives, you can imagine a bunch of elite performers sitting around and talking about their biggest failures and most beneficial errors. You can count on it that anyone who has risked and aspired to produce on a grand scale has also had some sizable mishaps and missteps. The momentary pain or embarrassment can be overcome with how it jettisons you to greater pinnacles.

Practices and Structures

With new tricks for goal setting and a fresh perspective on what happens when you don't achieve your goals, there are some very practical tips and tools to bring you success in all areas of ALIVEness. Two of your biggest allies are practices and structures.

"People rely on intelligence to solve problems, and they are naturally baffled when comprehension proves impotent to effect emotional change. To the neocortical brain, rich in the power of abstractions, understanding makes all the difference, but it doesn't count for much in the neural systems that evolved before understanding existed. Ideas bounce like so many peas off the sturdy incomprehension of the limbic and reptilian brains. The dogged implicitness of emotional knowledge, its relentless unreasoning force, prevents logic from granting salvation just as it precludes self-help books from helping. The sheer volume and variety of self-help paraphernalia testify at once to the vastness of the appetite they address and their inability to satisfy it" (Lewis, Amini, & Lannon, 2000, p. 118; You may be having a moment of déjà vu; you did read this

quotation six [or one in this case] chapters ago. Isn't it funny that we know one of the best ways to learn is through repetition, but we fear repeating ourselves? I was going to remove this quotation when I realized I had used it previously, but better to make this bonus teaching point: it is valuable to say things more than once; it's okay to repeat yourself; although you may feel like you are becoming redundant and going on too long and maybe your audience is starting to feel the same way, you may actually be, in spite of their slight irritation, helping to bring home a good point).

By this point, you should be convinced that knowing what to do is insufficient as the source of effective and consistent action. What you actually do on a regular basis can alter who you are. We have seen over time and with various groups, that you don't have to like it, but if you keep practicing, you will produce results.

Practices are the magic of regular contributions to shifting who you are and what you accomplish. It seems everyone has heard about the 10,000 hours that are reported to be required to become an expert. Those hours accumulate through steady practice. Make some passionate commitments to taking daily steps in the direction of what you value most. Anything you do every day or almost everyday shapes who you become. Some actions may be unintentional habits. If you select items mindfully and follow through regularly, you will produce beneficial results.

Structures are the reminders that support you in taking the actions. The human memory is quite faulty and it is folly to rely on your good intentions to see you through to persistent action. A structure could be as simple as a daily alarm in your smartphone.

Anything that exists outside of your brain, preferably that will do something to grab your attention (like make a sound or flash) can be a useful structure. You can be creative and have fun with structures. You might paste a picture or saying on your bathroom mirror – knowing that when you see it everyday it will serve to have you complete a practice. You might make a point of ending your day by putting your exercise clothes where you will trip over them in the morning as a reminder to exercise.

Please don't be confused by the relative simplicity of practices and structures. The difference between going forward with a head full of interesting ideas and insights and truly creating a life of ALIVEness is highly based on the extent to wish you implement the gems from this chapter. Please take the time to *feel* the juice of connecting with your strengths and priming your motivational pump. Use the AMP and MTO methods and *write* down your goals. Absolutely select at least one practice and one supporting structure that you can count on doing regularly. Really. Like if you had to promise that if you didn't complete your practice regularly during the upcoming week, you'd have to chop off one of your arms. Another great structure is to have a friend, "committed listener," "accountability buddy," or a coach with whom you will share your plans and have a clear communication of precisely what you will do by when and how you will report in.

Knowing is not enough, we must apply.
Willing is not enough, we must do. (Bruce Lee)

References

Amabile, T., & Kramer, S. J. (2011). *The progress principle*. Boston: Harvard Business School Publishing.

Lewis T., Amini F., & Lannon R. (2000). *A general theory of love*. New York: Random House.

McKee, A. (1991). *Individual differences in planning for the future*. Unpublished PhD Dissertation. Case Western Reserve University.

Weick, K.E. & Sutcliffe, K. M. (2007). *Managing the unexpected* (2nd ed.). San Francisco: Jossey-Bass.

[1]I acknowledge my colleagues at InspireCorps for their contribution to these ideas about Performance Goal Setting: Priming Motivation and AMP Goals

[2] I first heard about MTO goals from Raymond Aaron (2008)

CONCLUSION
FOR THOSE WHO DARE TO TEACH

I hope you enjoyed the bonus chapters and I look forward to sharing the rest of *ALIVE!* with you in the coming months. Please stay in touch.

Yes, I believe it takes courage to be a teacher and I do feel that those of us who dare to engage in this challenging and rewarding human enterprise should continue to be lifelong learners. This is more than attending required events for continuing education credits. What is essential is never ceasing to grow and develop as a person; to engage in personal development to **be** the best teacher you can be and "put aside your formal theories, intellectual constructs, axioms, statistics, and charts when you reach out to touch that miracle called the individual human being" (Louis Schmier, 1995).

I've heard it said that the greatest gift you can give is to allow someone to make a difference with you. Thank you for this opportunity to share my experiences and ideas with you. I sincerely hope that this book inspires you and your teaching and that it assists you as students grant you an opportunity to be of service to them.

Please be in touch with your comments, suggestions, questions, and ideas.

Namaste.
Billy

billy@billystrean.com
www.exhilaratedperformance.com
Twitter: @billystrean
LinkedIn: www.linkedin.com/in/billystrean
Faceboook: fb.me/ExhilaratedPerformance

ABOUT THE AUTHOR

A former three-sport NCAA athlete and coach, Dr. Billy Strean has a doctorate in sport and exercise psychology from the University of Illinois.

He is a Master Somatic Coach (Strozzi Institute), Registered Yoga Teacher, Certified Laughter Yoga Teacher, and Certified Professional Co-active Coach. It is precisely this eclectic range of disciplines and fields of study — somatics, yoga, sport psychology, laughter and play, and his 30+ years of teaching experience — that is the foundation of Dr. Strean's success both in the classroom as well as outside the classroom as keynote speaker and workshop facilitator.

In 2008, Dr. Strean received the University of Alberta's Rutherford Award for Excellence in Undergraduate Teaching. In 2011, Dr. Strean was one of ten Canadians selected to join the prestigious 3M National Teaching Fellowship. His recent audio book, *Humor Me: Lighten Up and Love Life Laughing*, explores the benefits of laughter and humour and how to apply them in daily life. Through his company, Exhilarated Performance, Billy has provided over 500 dynamic presentations across North America to help people to Re-Charge. Re-Connect. Re-Discover.

79408373R00050

Made in the USA
Columbia, SC
31 October 2017